# WOMEN OF FAITH™
## STUDY GUIDE SERIES

# CONTAGIOUS JOY

## BY

# CHRISTA KINDE

## FOREWORD BY

# PATSY CLAIRMONT

## NELSON IMPACT
### A Division of Thomas Nelson Publishers
*Since 1798*

www.thomasnelson.com

Published by Nelson Impact, a Division of Thomas Nelson, Inc., P.O. Box
141000, Nashville, Tennessee, 37214.

ISBN-10: 1-4185-2789-0
ISBN-13: 978-1-4185-2789-1

06 07 08 EB 7 6 5 4 3 2 1

# ✦ CONTENTS ✦

# ✦ FOREWORD ✦

*Contagious: Spreading or tending to spread from one to another; catching.*

*Joy: A condition or feeling of high pleasure or delight.*

I love when one unexpected word comes together with another unexpected word, and in the marriage of the two, they bring us a whole new dimension of understanding—like in the case of *contagious* and *joy.*

*Contagious* for me always brings to mind my sons, who during their childhood, were riddled with measles, chicken-pox, or some other illness. Then there were the annual notes from school warning parents of outbreaks of head lice, which prompted me to dig through their curly locks in search of trouble.

Instead of connecting *contagious* and *disease,* how refreshing to think of *contagious* teamed with *joy.* Then instead of fearing an outbreak, we'd embrace *contagious,* because who do you know wouldn't love a case of contagious joy?

We believers have the commission to spread joy in this world in order to combat the insidious spread of hopelessness. Now don't misunderstand—when I say *spread,* I don't mean like smearing peanut butter across a slice of bread. I don't mean that we should try to apply joy onto others. No, true joy spreads as we live out God's way in our lives with such cred-ibility that others move closer to purposely catch it.

I don't think there are many qualities that are as winsome as joy. Think about it…do you know a joyous person? Do you not want to be with them at every opportunity? I know I do.

Joy-people are popular, in demand, hired first, applauded, appreciated, and sought out. Joy makes hard days easier, dark days brighter, optimism possible, and friendships a pleasure.

My friend Mary Graham, the president of Women of Faith, is a pleasure and an authentic joy bubble. She radiates warmth, demonstrates faith, and her perspective on even difficulties is a bright lantern. I have seldom, if ever, seen Mary stuck in the muck of daily challenges or entwined in the webs of ornery folks. Joy has created a large space in her heart for a diversity of people whom she receives with unbridled enthusiasm. I have watched Mary choose to believe the best and leave the rest to the Lord.

I say, sign me up for a big fat case of that!

Actually, that's what you have decided to do when you commit yourself to this study, because it has been written in such a way that the truth will cause us to sidle up to joy and learn from it. And trust me—joy is an appealing teacher.

And I'm not talking about any syrupy substitute of overdone niceness—yuk! I'm speaking of joy that burbles up from your relationship with Christ. Joy that will cause your toes to tap, your heart to giggle, your dreams to return, your spirit to be refreshed, your vision to expand, and your dance card to fill. And what fun to have a case of something others want! You won't have to convince others about joy, because joy will cast her net of authenticity and draw in even the reluctant. Joy is just that appealing.

So, sharpen your pencil, open God's Word, and get ready. You're about to break out into contagious joy! May you never recover!

*Joyfully,*
*Patsy*

# ✦ INTRODUCTION ✦

*"A twinkle in the eye means joy in the heart."*
—Proverbs 15:30 MSG

You're walking down the street on a dreary, drizzly day. Everything is gray and gloomy, damp and disheartening. Shoulders hunched against the wet, you slog ahead in a dismal funk. Then, something catches your interest. Your ears pick up the sound of a cheerful whistle just ahead. To your astonishment, you're confronted with a woman in a luminescent yellow raincoat and bright green galoshes toting a polka-dot umbrella. Her spirits are obviously undampened by the inclement weather. In fact, she appears to be dancing to her own tune right between the raindrops. Suddenly, she takes a mighty leap, landing in a particularly large puddle and making a satisfying *ker-splash*. A smile tugs at your own lips. You can't help it. This gal's joy is contagious!

Joy has a way of working its way from the inside out. When our lives are filled with joy, we turn heads, too! The symptoms are unmistakable. A twinkle in the eye. A ready smile. A skip in the step. A song in the heart. Joy lends a glow to the face and a lilt to the voice. Joyful people whistle while they work and break into spontaneous song. And joy is contagious. So, what about you? Would you be diagnosed as a puddle plodder, or a puddle jumper?

Yearning for a more joyful outlook on life? Joy is the birthright of every believer, but rainy days have a way of distracting us from that fact. In this study, we'll take a careful look at this uniquely Christian characteristic. We have every reason to be joyful. We can express our inner joy in numerous ways. We can even hang onto joy when other emotions clamor through our hearts. Joy can have the effect of effervescence, exuberance, exhilaration, and enthusiasm. Joy is our strength and our song. It provides a solid foundation in our hearts. And although joy isn't exactly the same as happiness or glee, it leads conveniently into them. Joy is infectious, transmittable, spreadable, and catching. In a word, joy is contagious!

*"I'm whistling, laughing, and jumping for joy;*
*I'm singing your song, High God."*

**Psalm 9:2** MSG

CHAPTER 1

# JOYLESS LIVING

### "ALL THE JOY IS GONE FROM OUR HEARTS.
### OUR DANCES HAVE TURNED INTO DIRGES."

**Lamentations 5:15 MSG**

Our house is like most houses where a child is in residence. After several years' worth of birthdays and Christmases, we have a remarkable accumulation of toys. Stuffed animals, board games, coloring books, baby dolls, train sets, puzzles, cars, kitchen toys, picture books, building blocks. I usually buy books for the kids, but grandpas and grandmas, aunties and uncles are always finding excuses to add to our abundance. You would think this profusion would give any child delight—endless possibilities for all manner of play. But what do we hear? "I'm bored."

There are times when our spiritual lives are no different. We are surrounded by all of God's goodness and blessings. By

## CLEARING
## + THE +
## COBWEBS

Did you have a favorite toy when you were a child?

all rights we should be content and happy. Still, a restlessness, a bore-dom, and the conviction that something is missing settles around us. Like a whiney child, we scuff our feet and grumble, "I'm bored." Despite everything we have to be thankful for, we find no joy in our days.

**1.** Joyless living is aptly described in Proverbs 23:29. Please fill in the blanks.

"Who has _____?

Who has _____?

Who has _____?

Who has _____?

Who has _____ without _____?

Who has _____ of _____?"

**–Proverbs 23:29** NKJV

**2.** What has happened to the joy of the people in Isaiah 24:11?

*Our longings have the power to draw us to God in a passionate, desperate way that nothing else can.*

Nicole Johnson

**3.** What are the signs that joy is absent in Isaiah 24:8?

**4.** This theme is repeated in these next two verses. In each case, what lack is a symptom of joyless living?

• Ezekiel 26:13

• Psalm 137:2

**5.** There's a distinct difference between those who are God's own and those who are not. How does Isaiah 65:14 contrast the two?

ircumstances have a way of conspiring to leech the joy right out of our days. Even though we know joy is our rightful heritage from the Lord, we live as if we have never known joy's presence. We long for joy as if it were something far off and unobtainable. But joy isn't really a matter of receiving something new, but of discovering what has always been there. For believers, sometimes discovering joy is simply a matter of opening our eyes to a new way of seeing.

**6.** When joy slips from our view, we can pray for its return. What is the psalmist's prayer in Psalm 51:8?

> *I need to be drawn out of my own little world, and so do you. I see women all the time who seem joyless and lonely—I can see it in their expressionless eyes.*
>
> Nicole Johnson

**7.** Feelings are tricky things. We may know that joy can be ours but still not really feel very joyful. This can be hard to explain to others, but what does Proverbs 14:10 remind us by way of reassurance?

**8.** If joy is a matter of finding a new way of seeing, we can ask the Lord to show us the way into joy.

• What does David pray for in Psalm 16:11?

• What does Psalm 25:4 ask the Lord to do?

• In Psalm 119:18, what does the psalmist ask God for?

> *We all have seen dreams turn to ashes—ugly things, hopeless experiences—but beauty for ashes is God's exchange. In the midst of the darkness, you will learn lessons you might never have learned in the day.*
>
> Barbara Johnson

**9.** As with anything in which the Lord has a hand, there is hope. What promise do we find in Psalm 30:5?

## DIGGING DEEPER

Some days it's harder than others to draw upon the joy that we know is ours. Troubles and trials have a way of distracting us from it. Rediscovering our joy often means looking at things differently. God can open our eyes to His joy. The Bible talks a lot about the opening of eyes in order to see something that has always been there.

- Numbers 22:31
- Psalm 146:8
- Acts 26:18
- Psalm 119:18
- Luke 24:31

# PONDER & PRAY

Are you having trouble finding joy in your days? This is the perfect week to begin asking the Lord to open your eyes to His joy. Pray for a new way of seeing. Ask God for a joy that's unaffected by the changes in your circumstances or your emotions.

# TRINKETS TO TREASURE

At the close of every Women of Faith conference, women are asked to play a little game of pretend. Each conference guest is asked to imagine that a gift has been placed in her hands—one from each of the speakers—to serve as reminders of the different lessons shared. This study guide will carry on this tradition! At the close of each lesson, you will be presented with a small gift. Though imaginary, it will serve to remind you of the things you have learned. Think of it as a souvenir. Souvenirs are little trinkets we pick up on our journeys to remind us of where we have been. They keep us from forgetting the path we have traveled. Hide these little treasures in your heart, for as you ponder them, they will draw you closer to God.

## TRINKET TO TREASURE

We'll begin our collection of trinkets with a pair of glasses. These will serve as a reminder to you that you need never be trapped in a joyless life. Joy is yours. Sometimes all you have to do is ask the Lord to help you see it.

### ✦ NOTES & PRAYER REQUESTS ✦

## ✦ Notes & Prayer Requests ✦

# Turning Sorrow to Joy

### "I'll convert their weeping into laughter, lavishing comfort, invading their grief with joy."

**Jeremiah 31:13** MSG

Most toddlers have the uncanny knack for turning on and off faucets. We're not talking about the kitchen sink here. We're talking tears. Crocodile tears. One second, they're engulfed in misery. Piteous weeping communicates the sadness that overwhelms them. But in another moment, the heart-wrenching sobs can dissolve into smiles. Just like that, their sorrow is turned to joy.

Our own sorrow as adults is never so simple to alleviate. Sadness, dissatisfaction, depression, boredom—they're not easy to turn on and off. But God's promise is that we need never linger in joyless living. When our life is as flat and

## Clearing ✦ the ✦ Cobwebs

Have you ever had a makeover? Did you take before and after pictures?

gray as ashes, God invites us to exchange these ashes for the beauty of joy.

**1.** The story of joy begins with a sudden change. It's a matter of before and after. How does the "before" look according to these verses?

• Job 16:16

• Job 17:7

• Proverbs 15:13

**2.** But the promise is that joy can be ours. What does Psalm 126:6 say about the change from sorrow to joy?

*Joy must be the shocking pink thread in our tapestry, because people seem stunned by this flamboyant stitch. When we exhibit joy during trying times, others view us as odd ducks, 'cause everyone knows life ain't no ride on no pink duck.*

Patsy Clairmont

**3.** What does Isaiah 52:9 bid us to do?

**4.** How does Jeremiah describe the turned tables of sorrow and joy?

"Then shall the virgin _____ in the _____, And the young men and the old, together; For I will _____ their _____ to _____, Will _____ them, And make them _____ rather than _____." –Jeremiah 31:13 NKJV

**5.** This message is so encouraging, it bears repeating. What does Isaiah 35:10 tell us we will obtain?

> *Joy gives me calm assurance even though I go through the valley of the shadow of death. Joy enables me to hold my peace when people say and do ugly things to me. When we go through troubles, afflictions, persecutions, danger, illness, and distress, when the enemy comes to steal, kill, and destroy, we can have genuine joy in our hearts.*
>
> Thelma Wells

*W*hen a woman gets a makeover, she's hoping for transformation. She sees herself as ordinary, and hopes that the expertise of stylists and makeup artists will cause her hidden beauty to shine forth. But all the exfoliation, rehydration, and application in the world can only do so much. They only serve to polish up the exterior a bit. If we want to experience a real transformation, we need to start from the inside out. When God's joy fills our heart, it is so much more effective than mud packs, salt scrubs, and essential oils. Joy bestows on us a beauty that radiates from within.

**6.** God's exchange rate always seems to be tipped in our favor. What does He offer to us if we give Him our sorrows?

**7.** Joy is the ultimate transformation in our hearts. What does Isaiah compare it to in Isaiah 51:3?

**8.** When do we discover that joy resides in our hearts? What does the prophet say in Isaiah 12:3?

*Belonging to Jesus Christ means you've been given a heart transplant. With a new heart, He gives the power to be joyful, exuberant, and thankful.*

Barbara Johnson

9. Those who are lost discover joy when they are saved. Those who already belong to the Lord have only to rediscover the joy that already belongs to them.

•What does David pray in Psalm 51:12?

## DIGGING DEEPER

When we're overwhelmed by sorrow, worry, grief, or confusion, it seems as if we'll never see joy again. But God is full of surprises, and the impossible is well within His reach. Scripture says that we can hope, and joy will be ours again.

- Job 8:21
- Psalm 126:2

## PONDER & PRAY

No matter how dark a night you might have experienced, there is a promise that joy will come in the morning. Sorrow will not last forever. God is able to turn all our sadness into dancing and all our ashes into radiant beauty. Thank God for the joy you have now and for the joy He's promised to give to you when you need it most.

## TRINKET TO TREASURE

God offers to trade all our ashes for beauty. This transformation is better than any beauty treatment, so our trinket for the week is a makeup brush. Joy works its miracle on our lives from the inside out, and the results are lovely to behold!

### ✦ NOTES & PRAYER REQUESTS ✦

# CHAPTER 3

# A REASON FOR REJOICING

## "REJOICE BECAUSE YOUR NAMES ARE WRITTEN IN HEAVEN."

### Luke 10:20 NKJV

*I* wonder if Alice, whose adventures in Wonderland have become well known, looked back at the moment she decided to follow that White Rabbit as a turning point in her life. After that, her life was completely changed. And how about Cinderella? Which event changed her life more—the day her father died and she became a slave in her own home, or the day the prince fitted a glass slipper onto her foot and made her his bride? Do you think Humpty Dumpty is still kicking himself for deciding to climb that wall? Does Peter Rabbit wish he'd never disobeyed his mother and entered Mr. McGregor's garden?

## CLEARING ✦ THE ✦ COBWEBS

Do you have an event or a decision in your life that became so monumental that you find yourself wondering what would have happened if you'd chosen differently? What is your *what if?*

When we look at these kinds of occurrences, we can clearly see a before and after. *Before*, life was this way, but *after*, this is the way we lived. As a matter of fact, all of history turns on one choice, one event. When God chose to send His Son to live and die for our redemption, everything changed. Jesus' coming, death, and resurrection are the most pivotal events ever. Without Jesus, we would never have a reason for rejoicing.

**1.** What does Job 20:5 say about the good times of the godless?

**2.** Joy is found in the Lord. Throughout the Old Testament, the prophets foretold of a time when joy would brim over for God's people. What did Isaiah prophesy in Isaiah 9:2–3?

**3.** In Luke 1:14, what does God's messenger say will bring joy and gladness?

> *Joy is permanent. Once you have it, you never lose it. It may be overshadowed by human frailties, but real joy lasts for eternity.*
>
> Thelma Wells

**4.** In Luke 2:10, this most familiar of passages, what fulfillment of the promise of joy is heard proclaimed?

**5.** Only God's chosen people were looking for the Messiah to come. But joy in Christ's coming was not limited to the Jews. From the very beginning, who rejoiced in the fulfillment of God's promise?

There are plenty of good reasons for celebrating. Opening night. Promotions. Windfalls. New babies. Graduation. Letters of acceptance. Birthdays. Generally speaking, the bigger the reason for rejoicing, the bigger the party we throw. While a card in the mail was satisfactory for Grandma's 73rd, 76th, and 79th birthdays, a bigger celebration was called for when her 80th rolled around. For Christians, we have the biggest reason ever for rejoicing. We rejoice because we have God's love and the hope of eternal life with Him.

6. Jesus' coming brought all of us the hope of joyful living. In His parables, Jesus said that what He brought, the kingdom of heaven, was a treasure. How does the man in Matthew 13:44 react when he discovers this eternal gift?

7. While Jesus' coming was certainly a fulfillment of God's promise, few understood that His death was needed to secure our joy. How did Jesus attempt to explain this to His disciples in John 16:20?

*As women who have been drawn close to the heart of God by the embrace of Christ, you and I have the best reason of all to rejoice.*

Sheila Walsh

**8.** After Jesus' resurrection, joy upon joy unfolded in the lives of His followers.

- Sometimes we're a little afraid of the joy we experience. In Matthew 28:8, what was mingled with the women's joy?

- What feelings overwhelmed the disciples in Luke 24:41?

- What does Luke 24:52 say that Jesus' friends and followers experienced?

> *Genuine versus counterfeit. Real versus fake. Long-lasting versus short-term. Joy versus happiness. The world didn't give me joy, and the world can't take it away.*
>
> Thelma Wells

**9.** Not only did the joy of Jesus' return change the lives of His follow- ers—it ended up changing the whole world. What does Acts 17:6 say about the early Christians?

## DIGGING DEEPER

Take a look at Isaiah's description of the joy in his soul. What might you compare with your own reason for rejoicing?

*"I will sing for joy in God, explode in praise from deep in my soul! He dressed me up in a suit of salvation, he outfitted me in a robe of righteousness, As a bridegroom who puts on a tuxedo and a bride a jeweled tiara."* **–Isaiah 61:10** MSG

## PONDER & PRAY

We don't just have joy, we have a very good reason for being joyful. It helps to remind ourselves of that. Spend some time this week pondering all the things over which you can rejoice—from the smallest of blessings to the greatest reason of all—God's amazing gift of salvation.

## TRINKET TO TREASURE

Jesus is indeed our greatest reason for rejoicing. His birth was heralded by good tidings of great joy. Usually we spend the month of December pondering this, but we're not limited to that timeframe. Our trinket for the week is a star, like the Bethlehem star that first bore witness to the most joyful tidings ever heard.

### ✦ NOTES & PRAYER REQUESTS ✦

# CHAPTER 4

# OUR HEARTS REJOICE IN HIM

### "GLORY IN HIS HOLY NAME; LET THE HEARTS OF THOSE REJOICE WHO SEEK THE LORD!"

**1 Chronicles 16:10** NKJV

There's an old song made famous by Frank Sinatra called, "I Only Have Eyes for You." Some of the lyrics say, "I don't know if we're in a garden/Or in a crowded avenue/You are here, so am I/Maybe millions of people go by/But they all disappear from view/And I only have eyes for you." When we give someone or something our full attention, everything else tends to fade into the background. For a while, at least, nothing else matters.

We experience joy in our lives because of the Lord, and our hearts rejoice in Him. Our joy pours out in songs, gladness, praise, and worship. That's when everything else fades into the background, as we focus our rejoicing on the One who brings us joy. That reminds me of another song:

## CLEARING ✦ THE ✦ COBWEBS

Do you have something you would describe as your "pride and joy"?

"When I look into Your holiness/When I gaze into Your loveliness/ When all things that surround become shadows in the light of you/I worship You, I worship You/The reason I live is to worship You."

**1.** Our joy is tied up with the Lord. He is our Source of joy and our reason for rejoicing. What does David urge us to do in Psalm 5:11?

**2.** The Lord brings joy to our hearts. Our hearts rejoice because of Him. What imagery does Jeremiah 31:12 use to describe the life of one who finds joy in God?

**3.** David wrote, "Our hearts brim with joy since we've taken for our own his holy name" (Ps. 33:21 MSG). Each of us rejoices in the Lord because of the way in which He wooed and called us to Himself. Every story is unique and personal. What is yours?

*It is quite possible you have the thought that Luci Swindoll promotes a philosophy which says, "To celebrate life, one must skip around with a giddy grin on one's face, always encountering every situation with a smile (at worst) or an attitude of hilarity (at best)." I can understand how you might think that...but what I'm trying to convey is much more profound than that....Joy is not just written on our faces, it must be living in our spirits. Therein lies a vast difference.*

Luci Swindoll

**4.** According to Ecclesiastes 2:26, what does God give to His own?

**5.** What does Solomon say God does in our hearts in Ecclesiastes 5:20?

When someone has something that gives them great pleasure and satisfaction, it's sometimes referred to as their "pride and joy." I had a neighbor once whose car was his pride and joy—he spent hours washing and waxing it every weekend. Another neighbor finds great satisfaction in her rose garden, where she putters for hours every week. Yet another neighbor works tirelessly to maintain his pride and joy—a perfectly manicured lawn. Our pride and joy tends to be that thing on which we shower the bulk of our time, attention, and affection. It's the thing we focus on the most.

Have you ever thought that God could be—not necessarily your *pride* and joy—but your joy? He can and will be our sole source of joy as we spend our time with Him.

**6.** Just knowing Jesus should bring joy to our souls. But what does Deuteronomy 26:11 say is another facet of our relationship with God that can bring joy?

**7.** Hannah had good reason for joy. In her thankfulness to the Lord for the blessing of a child, joy overflowed into praise.

"My _____ _____ in the _____; My horn is _____ in the LORD. I _____ at my enemies, Because I _____ in Your _____." –1 Samuel 2:1 NKJV

> *I find that my joy is enlarged by understanding that as a child of God, even my pain has purpose. That realization doesn't eliminate my pain, but it makes it more manageable, allowing me other emotions in the midst of calamity, including shocking pink joy.*
>
> Patsy Clairmont

**8.** What is another way in which our hearts find a reason for rejoicing, according to Jeremiah 15:16?

**9.** Nehemiah 8:12 echoes Jeremiah's words. Why have the people begun to celebrate and rejoice greatly in this passage?

# DIGGING DEEPER

*Light-seeds are planted in the souls of God's people, joy-seeds are planted in good heart-soil.* **–Psalm 97:11** MSG

The Bible speaks about the state of our hearts and the joy that can fill it. For a little extra investigation this week, consider the passages surrounding Matthew 13:20 and Luke 8:13. What brings lasting joy?

# PONDER & PRAY

God brings joy into our lives by many means—answered prayers, wisdom, His Word, good gifts, manifold blessings. All these things bring our hearts to rejoicing. "When the righteous see God in action they'll laugh, they'll sing, they'll laugh and sing for joy" (Ps. 68:3 MSG). God should be our joy, and all else should fade out of focus in His light.

## Trinket to Treasure

When it comes to joy, the Lord should be our focus. He's our source of joy, and in His presence everything else just disappears from view. Our hearts are intent on Him as we worship God. To remind us of this, our trinket this week will be an eraser. It'll remind us of how everything else fades away in His presence.

### ✦ Notes & Prayer Requests ✦

# CHAPTER 5

# SING FOR JOY OF HEART

"BEHOLD, MY SERVANTS SHALL SING FOR JOY OF HEART."

**Isaiah 65:14** NKJV

Emotions were never meant to be bottled up inside. When we try to contain them, the pressure builds. Usually, we think of this mounting accumulation of strong feelings in negative ways. Too often, suppressed anger builds until it boils over in rash deeds and scathing words. The sadness we attempt to hide will lead to a storm of tears. When we try to keep our fears under wraps, they can mount up until we're in a panic. But have you ever considered that our other good emotions tend to spill over into our lives, as well? Take joy, for example. When our hearts are filled with joy to the point of overflowing, it bubbles over. And how do

## CLEARING ✦ THE ✦ COBWEBS

Have you ever poured vinegar over baking soda? What happens if you do?

we express this abundant joy? According to Scripture, we sing for joy of heart.

**1.** In Jeremiah 25:10, the prophet says that every sound of joy will be banished from the land. What examples of these joyful sounds does Jeremiah list?

**2.** We are not alone in our joy and rejoicing. What else does Isaiah 55:12 say will break forth into song in the joy of worship?

**3.** In 1 Chronicles 16:31–33, what else rejoices before the Lord?

**4.** What sings for joy in Job 38:7?

> *Our family enjoys good gospel music. We have discovered that praising God in song lifts our spirits, clears our heads, and opens a place for the Holy Spirit to speak to us.*
>
> Thelma Wells

**5.** We lift up our voices in joyful shouts and songs of worship. But in our creative capacity, people have added to the variety of joyful noises we can make. What does Job 21:12 say can accompany our rejoicing?

My husband has been in various choirs and musical groups since he was a mere lad. He's a good singer and an asset to any bass section, but he's confessed to a bit of mischief over the years. On one particular occasion, the choir he was in was supposed to perform a piece which he'd somehow neglected to memorize. Since he didn't know the words and didn't want to stand there with his mouth shut, he came up with Plan B. Eyes fixed on the director, and with beatific attentiveness, he mouthed "Watermelon, watermelon, watermelon…" in time to the music. No one was the wiser!

If the joy in our hearts is going to spill over into song, it'd be helpful to know the words. Keep a hymnal handy. Print out the lyrics to praise choruses. Put the words to all five verses of that old hymn on a sticky note by the sink, and memorize the words as you tidy the kitchen. Find excuses to sing for joy of heart!

**6.** Where does the psalmist say he will go to praise God in Psalm 43:4?

**7.** What sacrifice does David say he will bring to the Lord in Psalm 27:6?

> *When you're going through your daily routine or when you face trials and tribulations, do you allow music to comfort you? When times are good, do you sing for joy?*
>
> Thelma Wells

**8.** "The voice of _____ and the voice of _____, the voice of the _____ and the voice of the _____, the voice of those who will say: '_____ the _____ of hosts, For the _____ is _____, For His _____ endures _____'—and of those who will _____ the _____ of _____ into the _____ of the LORD." –Jeremiah 33:11 NKJV

> *God enjoys the song we lift up in praise to Him. He even reciprocates by singing back to us, as the verse in Zephaniah tells us, "He will rejoice over you with singing"* (3:17 NKJV).
>
> Thelma Wells

**9.** What does Psalm 33:3 encourage us to do?

## DIGGING DEEPER

Take a look at Luke 19:37–40. What does this passage tell us about praise?

## PONDER & PRAY

This week, don't just ponder the joy you have in the Lord. Let it overflow! As you go through the week ahead, let your heart bubble over with praise. Put the prayers you pray to a tune. Break out a hymnal and learn the prayers of the past put to song. Sing for joy of heart!

## TRINKET TO TREASURE

We are told that if we won't give praise to the Lord, then the rocks will take over and do it for us! Our trinket this week is a stone. Put it somewhere where it can remind you to lift up your voice in joyful song!

### ✦ NOTES & PRAYER REQUESTS ✦

# ✦ Notes & Prayer Requests ✦

# CHAPTER 6

# RESOUNDING JOY

"DAVID SPOKE TO THE LEADERS OF THE LEVITES TO APPOINT
THEIR BRETHREN TO BE THE SINGERS ACCOMPANIED BY
INSTRUMENTS OF MUSIC, STRINGED INSTRUMENTS, HARPS, AND
CYMBALS, BY RAISING THE VOICE WITH RESOUNDING JOY."

**1 Chronicles 15:16** NKJV

Early in our marriage, my husband and I rented a house that was not too far from a small football stadium. The field was tucked into a largely residential area, and it was put to use by the peewee leagues, the local high schools, and even a semi-professional football team. It had bleachers, lights, and loudspeakers. In the fall months, we always knew if there was a game afoot. Even though we were six blocks away, the air would throb with the beat of drums. If the wind was blowing the right way, we would catch snatches of the other instruments in the marching band, too—trumpets, tubas, trombones. The cheering crowds, the

## CLEARING ✦ THE ✦ COBWEBS

Were you in a high-school band, choir, or both? What part did you sing? What instrument did you play?

amplified commentary, the referees' whistles, and the enthusiastic band made a resounding noise.

Our joy can be expressed in a resounding fashion, as well, if we lift up our voices with other believers in corporate worship. When our voices are raised together in song and praise, they carry all the way to heaven's throne.

*Want to lift your spirits from the hustle and bustle of the day? Sing to the Lord.*

Thelma Wells

**1.** What gave the psalmist joy, according to Psalm 122:1?

**2.** David joined the processions of people who made their way to the temple for worship each day. On Sabbath days and feast days, there would be cheerful crowds all winding their way through the city streets. "A procession of joy and laughter!" (Ps. 45:15 MSG). What memory does David share with us in Psalm 42:4?

**3.** What does Psalm 32:11 encourage us to do?

**4.** Who is expressing joy in Psalm 132:9?

*I've always enjoyed praising God in song, singing praise-and-worship songs has calmed me when I'm upset, adjusted my attitude when it gets out of whack, given me patience when I'm restless, and infused me with the sheer pleasure of making music to the Lord. I love to sing!*

Thelma Wells

**5.** What else raises a shout for joy in the Lord, according to Psalm 65:13?

*H*ave you ever attended a Women of Faith conference? The worship services during these gatherings are definitely prime examples of resounding joy. It's awesome to stand down on the floor and to look up into the tiers of seats rising all around. So many faces filled with joy. So many hands and voices raised. The sound is glorious as so many unite in adoration and praise.

**6.** What elements came together to create a resounding clamor of joy in 1 Chronicles 15:16?

**7.** How does 1 Kings 1:40 describe the joyful noise lifted up by God's people?

> *Joy is a Jesus song that He willingly sings into the human spirit.*
>
> Patsy Clairmont

**8.** On a much later occasion, God's people rejoiced. How is their sound described in Nehemiah 12:43?

**9.** What is the invitation of Psalm 35:27?

# DIGGING DEEPER

When we consider the resounding sound of corporate worship, we think not only of voices raised in joyful worship, but of the instruments that accompany us.

- 2 Samuel 6:5
- 1 Chronicles 23:5
- 1 Kings 10:12
- Psalm 33:2

# PONDER & PRAY

There are times when joy fills our hearts with a secret sweetness, but there are times when joy likes to get good and noisy! This week, when you ponder the joy of the Lord, don't keep it all to yourself. Get yourself into a group—family, friends, your church's choir or congregation—and add your voice to those of others in joyful praise.

# TRINKET TO TREASURE

Shouts of joy are like the thrumming of a marching band heard in the distance. You can hear the noise from far off as it resounds through the air. Since we can't take the whole kit and caboodle for a trinket, we'll settle for a drum this week. It'll be your instrument of praise as you join the rest of your comrades and strike up the band.

# CHAPTER 7

# JOY MINGLED

"WITH FEAR AND GREAT JOY."

–Matthew 28:8 NKJV

Have you ever been caught in a sun shower? I remember the very first time I was, as a young girl. One minute the sun was shining from clear skies. The next minute the sun was shining through a curtain of shimmering raindrops, falling from a startlingly blue sky. The rain was heavy—big, fat drops coming hard and fast—and every drop seemed to catch the light. I was caught in a sparkling curtain of incongruity. It was a little disconcerting at first. After all, everyone knows that sun and rain don't coexist!

Equally strange is the fact that joy can coexist with a wide range of seemingly incongruous emotions. In the midst of difficulties, in the company of uncertainty, in

## CLEARING ✦ THE ✦ COBWEBS

Some things taste better in combination—strawberries and rhubarb, oatmeal and brown sugar, pineapples and coconut. What's your favorite flavor combination?

57

the middle of grief, joy, mixed with whatever life brings our way, remains undiminished.

**1.** Does the presence of joy mean we'll never experience stress, fear, worry, guilt, or pain? Of course not. But when those other emotions plague us, joy isn't thrust out entirely. How does Paul describe joy's tenacity in 2 Corinthians 4:8–10?

**2.** Though it seems incongruous, joy becomes mingled with the other emotions we experience. It's always there, at the very foundation of our faith. What does Paul's joy stand up to, according to 2 Corinthians 7:4?

*Have you noticed that we are laughter and tears, dirges and dances, jubilations and consternations, hallelujahs and woes?*

Patsy Clairmont

**3.** Paul offers several puzzling contradictions in his experiences. His honesty about the feelings he experienced helps us to see how faith and feelings coexist. What does he contrast in 2 Corinthians 6:10?

> *That's the way it is with life. Things may be going well. You may be enjoying luxuries and success, prestige and power, good health and prosperity. Then storms roll in with sudden vengeance, and your ship begins to sink.*
>
> Thelma Wells

**4.** For what does Paul commend the church at Thessalonica in 1 Thessalonians 1:6?

**5.** What does Jesus urge us to do in Luke 6:23? Why?

*F*lavor combinations have gotten out of control. The other day I was in a convenience store, looking for a bottle of orange juice—just plain orange juice. A quick look showed a definite leaning toward blended juices. Cran-apple, strawberry kiwi, peach mango, berry-berry, carrot papaya, pineapple orange, guava raspberry. Some juices are blended into milk, yogurt, or iced tea now, too.

You may not like green tea in your lemonade or banana in your orange juice, but a measure of joy in our days can definitely make them sweeter.

**6.** Joy also mingles happily with the better attributes in our emotional capacities. What does the Spirit bring to fruition in our hearts besides joy, according to Galatians 5:22–23?

**7.** When is joy needed the most, as we're trusting God for His strength, according to Colossians 1:11?

**8.** Joy steadies us so that we don't lose heart in face of our big and little problems. In 2 Corinthians 4:16–18 (NKJV), why does Paul say we needn't lose heart?

Therefore we do not _____ _____ (We don't give in to joyless living).

Even though our _____ man is _____ (even when things are tough),

yet the _____ man (the real me that only God can see)

is being _____ day by day (refreshed, made strong).

For our _____ affliction (made inconsequential by its temporary nature),

which is but for a _____ (compared with the vastness of eternity),

> *Some days, I really get that joy stuff. I enter into the tasks set before me with gusto while my heart hums. But other days I'm too full of sadness or too full of myself, or too overwhelmed with responsibilities to have much space for joy.*
>
> Patsy Clairmont

is _____ for us (actually has a purpose)

a far more _____ (we gain something greater by it)

and _____ weight of _____ (there are everlasting rewards),

while we do not _____ at the things which are _____ (we can't trust our eyes),

but at the things which are _____ _____ (we hold on to them by faith).

For the things which are seen are _____ (stuff and struggles go away),

but the things which are not seen are _____ (hang on to the everlasting).

**9.** Losing heart is a lot like losing your joy. Paul often encouraged those who were serving the Lord not to lose the joy they had in Him. What does Paul encourage the faithful to do in Galatians 6:9?

# DIGGING DEEPER

Joy mingled. It's like saying, "On the one hand, I'm frustrated with today's load of inconveniences. But on the other hand, I know that all these things are temporary. My joy is untouched." Sometimes it helps to talk to ourselves in this way. David knew this. What does he say in Psalm 43:5?

# PONDER & PRAY

This week, ask the Lord to strengthen the foundations of joy in your life. That way, when rough times and unexpected emotions storm through, your joy will remain. Like faith, hope, and peace, joy is a gift of God to His beloved children. Thank Him for the stability it lends to your heart.

# TRINKET TO TREASURE

It's strange but true. Joy can be a constant in our lives, no matter what circumstances and emotions might be at work. To remind us of this, our trinket this week will be a raindrop. Just as a sun shower sets raindrops to sparkling, the storms in our lives can be brightened by joy's presence. Hang your raindrop where the sun can shine through it!

# ✦ NOTES & PRAYER REQUESTS ✦

# CHAPTER 8

# COUNT IT ALL JOY

"MY BRETHREN, COUNT IT ALL JOY WHEN
YOU FALL INTO VARIOUS TRIALS."

**James 1:2** NKJV

A child stands at the plate, bat at the ready. Her dad is on the mound, pitching slow and easy. It's batting practice, and he's trying to help his daughter improve her swing. Though he's patient, and continues to urge her on with encouraging words, she's tired and frustrated. A swing and a miss. She waited too long. She calls out, "That one doesn't count!" Another miss. She was ahead of the ball that time. "Let me try again!" A foul ball skitters into the backstop. The girl is close to tears. "That one doesn't count, either!" she shouts to her dad. So the father calls for a break and sits down with his arm around his dusty daughter's shoulders. "Honey, we're not keeping score

## CLEARING ✦ THE ✦ COBWEBS

Do you like to play all kinds of games just because they're fun, or do you really only like to play games you're good at?

here. If you miss, it doesn't mean you've failed. This is just practice. You can learn from the balls you miss, as well as from the balls you hit. They all count if they teach you something about the game. You'll be a better batter if you do."

As Christians, we often feel a kind of pressure to succeed. We want to get it right and give God the glory. But life has a tendency to throw curve balls. We're hit with something we never saw coming, and all we want to do is put it behind us. But God has a purpose, even in our struggling times. When we long to shout, "That didn't count! I want to try again," James says, "It counts!" What's more, count it all joy.

**1.** Jesus never promised that our lives would be easy. As a matter of fact, the New Testament seems unanimous in its assurance that we will have many trials throughout our lives.

**Acts 20:19** – "_____ the Lord with all _____, with many _____ and _____" (NKJV).

**1 Peter 1:6** – "Now for a _____ _____, if need be, you have been _____ by _____ _____" (NKJV).

**James 1:2** – "My brethren, _____ it all _____ when you _____ into _____ _____" (NKJV).

**2.** What does Jesus use to illustrate the passing nature of our trials in John 16:21?

> *We don't recognize the value in celebrating the strange twists, the difficulties, the so-called failures, when we really should...and could. We consider our flops or hard times a defeat, but in reality they are God's greatest compliments. They're transforming love gifts from a gracious heavenly Father.*
>
> Luci Swindoll

**3.** What does Jesus go on to promise in John 16:22?

**4.** When it comes to "counting it all joy," we need to have this same forward-thinking attitude. The trials we face will be worth the end result — the promised joy that lies ahead of us. What was Jesus willing to endure for the sake of future joy, according to Hebrews 12:2?

*C*an you imagine what it would be like if no one was willing to endure a little hardship? What if Noah had decided that the whole ark business was just too much work for a man nearing his retirement? What if Moses had quit and gone home after just three plagues? What if Joshua decided to tiptoe past Jericho? What if Esther was unwilling to reschedule a manicure? What if David had declared that he didn't like confrontations — especially with foreign giants? What if Solomon had asked for cash upfront? What if Daniel had decided it was easier to try to fit in?

**5.** The message that comes across for us seems to be, "Hang in there. It'll be worth it in the end." What does Paul say will be ours if we can endure, according to 2 Timothy 2:12?

> Women in the midst of crisis and tragedy have taught me that life's dance of joy can be done in the shadows as well as the sunshine. Joy actually sparkles in darkness, and like heavenly fireworks, joy doesn't require daylight and cloudless skies. In fact, the illuminating wonder of joy dazzles with contrast.
>
> Patsy Clairmont

**6.** The writers of Scripture offer us encouragement, hope, promises, and the legacy of a life after which we can pattern our own. Take a look at each of these scriptures on endurance, and match them with their location.

___ 1 Corinthians 4:12    a. I endure all things so that more can be saved

___ 2 Timothy 2:3    b. Endure God's chastening

___ 2 Timothy 2:10    c. Reviled, we bless; persecuted, we endure

___ 2 Timothy 4:5    d. We count them blessed who endure

___ Hebrews 12:7    e. Endure hardship as a good soldier

___ James 5:11    f. Endure afflictions

**7.** Press on! Don't give up! Stick with it! Why does Paul say we can actually glory in our tribulations, according to Romans 5:3–4?

*There is just something about knowing that my failures, others' failures, hardships, mistakes, losses, and pain have meaning. For me, that understanding eases some of the agony of life and encourages me to keep on keeping on.*

Patsy Clairmont

**8.** It can be difficult to understand why we're always being confronted with difficulties. "Counting it all joy" means trusting that God's plan is the best one. What does Psalm 19:8 have to say about the directions God chooses for us?

**9.** We are given a hint of what the joy at the end of our path will look like. What does John tell us is in our future, according to Revelation 21:4?

## DIGGING DEEPER

Though it takes a monumental shift in perspective, we, too, need to count it all joy. All our perseverance and endurance will result in both present joy and future joy. It all counts.

- Philippians 3:7–8
- James 1:2
- James 5:11

## PONDER & PRAY

This week ponder what it means to count your trials as joy. We each have different struggles, so personalize this concept. What's on your list? We all need eyes to see the bigger perspective in order to find joy in our trials. Pray that God will help you see things His way.

# TRINKET TO TREASURE

In God's way of thinking, everything that comes our way has a purpose. The things we'd rather forget or do over again might be the very things He's using to make us stronger, wiser and more trusting. We're to count it all joy, even when life throws us a curve ball, so our trinket this week will be a wiffle ball. It can remind you of batting practice, when everything that is pitched your way becomes a chance to learn and grow and strengthen your game.

## ✦ NOTES & PRAYER REQUESTS ✦

# CHAPTER 9

# REJOICE WITH ME

"WE HAVE GREAT JOY AND CONSOLATION IN YOUR LOVE,
BECAUSE THE HEARTS OF THE SAINTS HAVE
BEEN REFRESHED BY YOU, BROTHER."

**Philemon 1:7** NKJV

*I*'m a part of a caring little community. We're from all over the place, yet we all consider ourselves friends. Not a day goes by that we don't check in with each other. We're a chatty bunch on the whole. We crack jokes and laugh together. We ask questions and pose riddles to get one another thinking. We're unstinting in our compliments, shameless in our flattery, generous to a fault. We love to use our creativity to surprise each other. We keep each others' mailboxes filled with little delights. We encourage one another, inspire one another, trust one another, and rejoice with one another.

This is a good picture of what the Lord wants for Christians to experience within the Church. We're to form a strong

## CLEARING ✦ THE ✦ COBWEBS

Take a survey! How many pillows do you have in your home right now?

community—caring, encouraging, trusting. Have you formed a circle of friends from within your congregation—a Sunday-school class, Bible-study group, ministry team? Do you find excuses to surprise and encourage one another regularly? It's amazing how joy can flourish when joy is shared!

> *Heavenly Father, You are a God who upholds us, stabilizes us, and never tires of being there. May we lovingly hold each other up and keep each other from falling. Inspire and enable us to "be there" for each other as you are there for each of us.*
>
> Marilyn Meberg

**1.** What does Paul say would give him great joy in Romans 15:32?

**2.** What does Philemon 1:20 say accompanies the joy Paul derives from his friend?

**3.** Fellow believers and friends can be a source of great cheer in our lives. What does Psalm 133:1–3 have to say about this kind of refreshment?

*I love that about my partners in the Women of Faith conferences. We bebop all over the country watching out for each other. We serve one another joyfully, from the heart. When one of us is down, we rally to her. When one of us celebrates, we rejoice together. We're a team. We never anticipated this kind of bonding, but bonded we are.*

Luci Swindoll

**4.** What is the promise of Proverbs 11:25?

**5.** Paul gave his life in the service of others and of God. He never stinted, but worked to see the joy of every believer strengthened and sustained.

• What did Paul call his ministry team in 2 Corinthians 1:24?

• Why did Paul say he would remain with the new believers in Philippians 1:25?

• According to 1 Thessalonians 2:19–20, what is Paul's joy?

*O*ur family has a passion for pillows. They're one of life's little luxuries, and have become our secret extravagance. Each of us in our family has at least two pillows for sleeping. Then, there are the pillows in decorative shams and throw pillows. When our beds are made up, our headboards disappear behind the heaps! Downstairs there are decorative pillows on the chairs and couches. Then there are the big, bright floor cushions. Even the dogs have a few pillows scattered throughout the house.

One of my favorite pillows is the bolster pillow. It's that sausage-shaped pillow, perfect for the curve of your neck. *Bolster* means, "to support or prop up; to buoy or hearten." That's what friends are for! We bolster each other up with our caring, our encouragement, and our shared rejoicing.

**6.** Paul was unstinting in his compliments and lavish in his encouragement to the believers he'd developed friendships with over the years. He was frank in telling them, "You are my joy!" Match up these verses, which also talk about the joys of fellowship.

___ Proverbs 12:20          a. We rejoiced exceedingly more for Titus' joy

___ Proverbs 21:15          b. My brothers and sisters, my joy and crown

___ 2 Corinthians 2:3      c. It is a joy for the just to do justice

___ 2 Corinthians 7:13    d. Desiring to see you and be filled with joy

___ Philippians 2:2         e. Counselors of peace have joy

___ Philippians 4:1         f. Fulfill my joy by being like-minded

___ 2 Timothy 1:4          g. My joy is the joy of you all

**7.** What tool do we have that can spread the most joy to those around us, according to Proverbs 15:23 and Proverbs 18:4?

**8.** What is Paul's prayer for all believers in Romans 15:5–6?

*How can we love God with everything and our neighbor as ourselves if we do not sacrificially give of ourselves with joy? In looking for the big opportunities to "perform" as a Christian, how many small God-given opportunities to love with depth do we miss?*

Sheila Walsh

**9.** There's no denying that it can be difficult to live in harmony with other people. We're all so different, and those differences can sometimes stir up feelings of jealousy, resentment, dislike, disgruntlement, and the like. That's why Paul urged Christians to strive for harmony. What list of admonitions does he give in 2 Corinthians 13:11?

## DIGGING DEEPER

When we're sharing our joy with others, it might be wise to bear in mind the wise words of Solomon in Proverbs 27:14—especially before our morning coffee!

## PONDER & PRAY

Are you a part of a caring community right now? If not, ask the Lord to lead you into one, or even better to start one! Reaching out and sharing the joy we all have in the Lord is an important part of the Christian life. We are a community for sharing, encouraging, ministering, and worshiping together. Find small ways to reach out and bolster someone's joy and faith this week.

## TRINKET TO TREASURE

As we're finding ways to rejoice with one another this week, our trinket simply must be a bolster pillow. Plump it up and plunk it down somewhere you'll see it often. It'll remind you that we're all part of a community that God put together to bolster one another's faith and to rejoice together in Him.

### ✦ NOTES & PRAYER REQUESTS ✦

# CHAPTER 10

# JOY IS MY STRENGTH

"YOUR JOY WILL BE A RIVER OVERFLOWING ITS BANKS!"

**John 16:24** MSG

Joy is just one of the many gifts that God gives to His people. God gives us His love, and that love humbles us. God gives us faith, and faith makes us confident. God gives us His peace, and that peace makes us steady. God gives us His hope, and that hope makes us expectant. And God gives us His joy, and that joy makes us...strong? Of all the words we could use to describe the joy of the Lord, would *strong* be at the top of your list?

Consider this. We can know that God loves us. We can be certain of God's promises. We can trust God for peace in every situation. We can make lists of the historical facts that support our faith. We can begin each day wondering if this could be

## CLEARING ✦ THE ✦ COBWEBS

Do you usually think with your head or your heart?

the day our hope is fulfilled. But if we do not have joy in all these truths, they seem stale, distant, even dull. All the academic pursuit of the facts of Scripture won't change a life with the dynamic power that joy has. Joy is the vibrancy, the brightness, the effervescent quality that makes our faith contagious!

**1.** As believers, we already know that God is the source of our inner strength. He's even called by that name—*my Strength*—in the Scriptures.

**Psalm 59:17** – "To You, O my _____, I will _____ _____" (NKJV).

**Isaiah 49:5** – "I shall be _____ in the _____ of the LORD, And My _____ shall be My _____" (NKJV).

*It's good to let go and laugh when life is weighing you down. It won't change any of the circumstances you find yourself in, but when you can laugh at the antics of others, it helps to lighten the load.*

Sheila Walsh

**2.** Words of praise and thanksgiving have been lifted up for centuries because of the strength the Lord gives to those who look to Him.

____ Exodus 15:2          a. O LORD, my strength and my Redeemer

____ 2 Samuel 22:33     b. My God, my strength, in whom I will trust

____ Psalm 18:1           c. God is my strength and power

____ Psalm 18:2           d. I will love you, O LORD, my strength

____ Psalm 19:14         e. In the fear of the LORD is strong confidence

____ Proverbs 14:26    f. The name of the LORD is a strong tower

____ Proverbs 18:10    g. The LORD is my strength and song

**3.** We're taught from the time that we are little that the Lord lends us His strength. "We are weak, but He is strong." What does Paul tell us about God's strength in 2 Corinthians 12:9?

**4.** It doesn't sound odd to say that God is our strength. But what subtle twist does Nehemiah 8:10 give to this notion?

**5.** What does David say about strength and joy in Psalm 21:1?

*H*ow can the joy of the Lord be our strength? It gives us gumption to function. It keeps us going. It lends us wings. It supports our steps. It strengthens our resolve. It steadies our nerves. It galvanizes our determination. It lightens our load. It brightens our outlook. It lifts our hearts.

**6.** What does John 15:11 tell us about the joy the Lord gives us?

**7.** What do Isaiah 9:3 and Isaiah 29:19 say God is able to do to our joy?

**8.** Joy isn't always just a by-product of God's blessings. Joy is a source of strength in our lives, and Jesus gave it intentionally. What does He say about joy in John 17:13?

> *When we realize our days here matter, our pain has significance, and our choices are meaningful, we can step through the darkest of times with hope in our hearts. It's not that we don't waver, but even our inquiries have the potential, when we are seeking, to lead us to a stronger faith.*
>
> Patsy Clairmont

**9.** What promise can we hang onto concerning our joy, as found in Psalm 16:11?

> *Joy is durable. It holds up under hardship and often is showcased in life's distresses. Joy is contagious, as well.*
>
> Patsy Clairmont

## DIGGING DEEPER

John wanted every believer to know the transforming quality of joy, but he didn't stop there. He prayed that we would have not just joy, but full joy, abundant joy, joy overflowing!

- John 16:24
- 1 John 1:4
- 1 John 1:12

## PONDER & PRAY

There's an old jingle that goes, "Everything's better with Blue Bonnet on it!" In our lives, everything we have from the Lord is made even better by the presence of joy. Ask the Lord to teach your heart to rejoice in His many blessings. Ask Him to add joy to your life of faith so that your faith is made stronger. Then the joy of the Lord can be your strength, as well.

## TRINKET TO TREASURE

Joy makes everything it's paired with better! Take joy in love! Rejoice in hope! Find joy in God's peace. Live out your faith with joy. Though joy may not seem a great source of strength, its lifting effect makes us stronger. To celebrate joy's transforming power, we'll choose a balloon as our trinket. Balloons lift our hearts and make us smile. They transform anything ordinary into a celebration!

### ✦ NOTES & PRAYER REQUESTS ✦

_____

_____

_____

_____

_____

_____

_____

## ✦ NOTES & PRAYER REQUESTS ✦

# CHAPTER 11

# RADIANT JOY

### "THEN YOU SHALL SEE AND BECOME RADIANT, AND YOUR HEART SHALL SWELL WITH JOY."

**Isaiah 60:5** NKJV

Superheroes can be exciting because they have unique abilities. Some can fly—or at least leap tall buildings in a single bound. Others have heightened senses—hearing, sight, smell. Some are able to manipulate matter—fire, water, ice, stone, metal. Some superheroes can breathe underwater, run faster than the eye can follow, talk to animals, or walk through walls. What makes these slightly strange folks superheroes are their wardrobe choices (gotta love the capes and tights) and their decision to use their unique abilities to help other people.

What super power would you find most useful? The amazing ability to sort socks at lightning speed? An uncanny

## CLEARING ✦ THE ✦ COBWEBS

If you could have any super power at all, what would you choose?

knack for balancing a checkbook to the penny every time? The power of navigation, allowing you to reach your destination without the use of maps? The gift of picking a perfect cantaloupe every time—perfectly sweet, never too green or too ripe? Or how about the super ability of reading illegible handwriting? Or super strong fingernails, so that your manicures last indefinitely and you never break a nail?

Actually, God's gifts are better than the imaginary gifts of comic book superheroes. We have the strength of joy on our side, and it's unshakeable, indestructible, invincible!

**1.** There's a reason that joy is joyful, and sometimes a purely academic study of joy loses sight of this. For that reason, I'm opening today's lesson with several verses about joy that are taken from the popular paraphrase, *The Message*. Feel free to comment on your favorite verses here!

> "More joy in one ordinary day Than they get in all their shopping sprees." —Psalm 4:7

> "I'm whistling, laughing, and jumping for joy; I'm singing your song, High God." —Psalm 9:2

"He's proved he's on my side; I've thrown my lot in with him. Now I'm jumping for joy, and shouting and singing my thanks to him." –Psalm 28:7

"God deals out joy in the present, the *now*." –Ecclesiastes 5:20

You'll see all this and burst with joy—you'll feel ten feet tall—as it becomes apparent that GOD is on your side." –Isaiah 66:14

"I'm singing joyful praise to GOD. I'm turning cartwheels of joy to my Savior God." –Habakkuk 3:18

"Their lives brimming with joy. Their children will get in on it, too—oh, let them feel blessed by GOD!" –Zechariah 10:7

**2.** What effect does joy have on us according to Isaiah 60:5?

*As we do the thing in front of us, joy comes. It multiplies and eventually hits us smack between the eyes, like a boomerang. It becomes a "hallelujah" in the choir loft of our mind. Joy is a treasure that multiplies by division.*

Barbara Johnson

**3.** To what does Psalm 19:5 compare joy?

**4.** The radiance of our joy is nothing compared to the radiance of God. How does Psalm 80:1 describe God?

> *Being touched by God's extravagant grace ignites something within us that causes others to notice. It's an interior glow that is like an exterior light in that it casts its influence in spite of the degree of darkness in which it finds itself—not only in spite of the darkness but also because of it. In the darkness the light becomes more attractive, more influential, more valuable, and more obvious.*
>
> Patsy Clairmont

**5.** What promise does Psalm 34:5 hold?

$\mathcal{W}$e have fairly simple parties whenever one of our children has a birthday. A family party at home with a few presents and a cake. When the candles are lit, the dining room light is turned out so that all eyes are turned to the face of the birthday boy or girl. Though they try to hide their grin of pleasure, their smile twinkles in their eyes. Sitting at the center of attention, basking in candle glow and blushing at our song, they are positively radiant.

Our joy in the Lord is just as radiant. It's unmistakable. It's irrepressible. It's irresistible. Nothing can hide the smile in the eyes of a joyful soul.

**6.** Jeremiah 31:12 describes our lives as radiant in the New Living Translation:

"They will come home and _____ _____ of _____ on the heights of Jerusalem. They will be _____ because of the many _____ the _____ has given them....Their _____ will be like a _____ _____, and all their _____ will be _____." –Jeremiah 31:12 NLT

**7.** What does Matthew 13:43 prophesy?

**8.** What lends to our radiance, according to Proverbs 4:22?

**9.** What does Jesus say gives us the radiance of a light-filled life in Luke 11:36?

## DIGGING DEEPER

We aren't the only ones who rejoice in radiance. Why are celebrations stirred up in the heavens, according to Luke 15:7–10?

## PONDER & PRAY

Brides and expectant mothers don't have a corner on radiance. Has someone ever stopped you to tell you that you're glowing? Ask the Lord to let His joy shine through your life this week. Thank Him for the light He lends to your soul!

## TRINKET TO TREASURE

Joy lends its radiance to the life of each believer. To remind you of this radiant joy, we'll choose a birthday candle as our trinket this week. Joy will make you shine forth like the sun itself when the Lord is with you.

*Each day the Lord gives us brings with it reasons to rejoice. Rejoice in this day the Lord has given you. He has joy waiting for you.*

Thelma Wells

# CHAPTER 12

# ENTERING JOY

### "EVERLASTING JOY SHALL BE THEIRS."

### Isaiah 61:7 NKJV

Summer is the time when all our hard work begins to bear fruit. Vegetables ripen on the vines. Berries come into season. Fruit trees are laden with a maturing harvest. Not so long ago, people depended on summer's bounty to see them through the winter months. Beans and peppers were dried. Vegetables were canned. Fruit went into row upon row of Mason jars. Potatoes and pumpkins went into root cellars. Pickles were brined. Jams and jellies sparkled by the pint. Herbs were hung in bunches from the rafters. By the time fall rolled around, the pantries, attics, storerooms, and cellars were bursting with

## CLEARING
## ✦ THE ✦
## COBWEBS

Do you have a favorite home-canned item?

stored food. Sacks, barrels, cans, jars—all filled. They held what was in store for the months ahead.

We are also waiting for what's in store. The joys our life on this earth holds are many, varied, and wonderful. They make us sing and dance and shout and glow. But for all their delights, every joy we've ever known is just a foretaste of what's in store for believers when we finally enter into joy.

**1.** While we have joy on this earth because of God, we can look forward to entering into joy when we see Him face to face. How do these verses describe such joy?

• Psalm 46:4

• Psalm 84:2

**2.** What does Isaiah 65:18 invite us to do?

> *We have not even begun to see what God has in store for us. Even the best moments that He showers on us are hardly the appetizer for the banquet He has prepared.*
>
> Sheila Walsh

**3.** Someday, all things will be made new. Joy will be a part of our future, too.

Isaiah 35:2 – "It shall _____ abundantly and _____, Even with _____ and _____" (NKJV).

Isaiah 65:18–19 – "Be _____ and _____ _____ in what I create; For behold, I create Jerusalem as a _____, And her people a _____. I will _____ in Jerusalem, And _____ in My people; The voice of weeping shall no longer be heard in her, Nor the voice of crying" (NKJV).

**4.** We've not seen Jesus face-to-face yet, but in believing, what do we receive?

*Hold onto your hats, girls, we've only just begun to experience all the delights God has prepared for us!*

Sheila Walsh

**5.** Where do we find fullness of joy according to Acts 2:28?

omething in our souls longs for the day. It's the moment we're all waiting for. Today's joys are just a hint of what awaits us. And so we live in the expectation of what's to come. Even now, Jesus is preparing a place for us with Him. When everything is ready, in God's perfect timing, we'll join our Lord in heaven. There, we'll find the proverbial porch light on. The red carpet will be rolled out, the welcome mat in place. And in that place, we'll find out what the fullness of joy is for those who belong to God.

**6.** What does Job 33:26 tell us brings joy?

> *Being touched by God's extravagant grace ignites something within us that causes people to notice. It's an interior glow that is like an exterior light in that it casts its influence in spite of the degree of darkness in which it finds itself—not only in spite of the darkness but also because of it. In the darkness the light becomes more attractive, more influential, more valuable, and more obvious.*
>
> Patsy Clairmont

**7.** When does 1 Peter 4:13 say our joy will be exceedingly great?

**8.** What are the words every believer longs to hear? What is the invitation we find in Matthew 25:21?

**9.** Let's take Jude 1:24 as a benediction to our study on the contagious joy that is ours.

> *From what I've heard,*
> *it doesn't get any*
> *better than Glory.*
>
> Patsy Clairmont

## DIGGING DEEPER

The invitation stands. The promises will be fulfilled. How do the following scriptures proclaim God's open arms?

- Psalm 118:20
- Acts 14:22
- Hebrews 10:19

- Matthew 7:21
- Hebrews 4:11
- Revelation 22:14

## PONDER & PRAY

Let your prayers this week be those of grateful expectation. Ponder His promises of future joy, and let the hope they bring fill your heart. No matter what this world brings to us, our future is secure with God. There will be joy. Radiant joy. Everlasting joy. Exceedingly great joy.

## TRINKET TO TREASURE

Our joy will be complete when we see our Lord face-to-face. He's preparing a place for us even now. When we are with the Lord, we'll actually be entering joy. The trinket we'll use to remind us of this great hope and promise is a welcome mat. When we cross that mat one day, we'll know joy in its fullest, most complete sense.

### ✦ NOTES & PRAYER REQUESTS ✦

_____

_____

_____

_____

_____

_____

_____

## SHALL WE REVIEW?

**Every chapter has added a new trinket to your treasure trove of memories. Let's remind ourselves of the lessons they hold for us!**

### 1. Glasses.

These serve as a reminder that you need never be trapped in a joyless life. Joy is yours. Sometimes all you have to do is ask the Lord to help you see it.

### 2. A makeup brush.

God offers to trade all our ashes for beauty. This transformation is better than any beauty treatment. Joy works its miracle on our lives from the inside out, and the results are lovely to behold!

### 3. A star.

Jesus is indeed our greatest reason for rejoicing. His birth was heralded by good tidings of great joy. Our trinket for the week is a star, like the Bethlehem star that first bore witness to the most joyful tidings ever heard.

### 4. An eraser.

When it comes to joy, the Lord should be our focus. He's our source of joy. Our trinket reminds us of how everything else fades away in His presence.

## 5. A stone.

We are told that if we won't give praise to the Lord, then the rocks will take over and do it for us! Our trinket this week is a stone. Let it remind you to lift up your voice in joyful song!

## 6. A drum.

Shouts of joy are like the thrumming of a marching band heard in the distance. A drum will be your instrument of praise as you join with other believers in joyful praise.

## 7. A raindrop.

Joy can be a constant in our lives, no matter what circumstances and emotions might be at work. Just as a sun shower sets raindrops to sparkling, the storms in our lives can be brightened by joy's presence.

## 8. A wiffle ball.

Everything that comes our way has a purpose. We're to count it all joy, even when life throws us a curve, so our trinket this week will be a wiffle ball. It can remind you of batting practice, when everything that is pitched our way becomes a chance to learn and grow and strengthen our game.

## 9. A bolster pillow.

As we're finding ways to rejoice with one another this week, plump up your pillow and plunk it down. It'll remind you that we're all part of a community that God put together to bolster one another's faith and to rejoice together in Him.

## 10. A balloon.

Joy makes everything it's paired with better! Though joy may not seem a great source of strength, its lifting effect makes us stronger. Just as balloons transform anything ordinary into a celebration, joy lifts our hearts and transforms our lives.

## 11. A birthday candle.

Joy lends its radiance to the life of each believer. Joy will make you shine forth like the sun itself when the Lord is with you.

## 12. A welcome mat.

Our joy will be complete when we see our Lord face-to-face. He's preparing a place for us even now. When we are welcomed into the presence of the Lord one day, we'll know joy in its fullest, most complete sense.

# WHAT SHALL WE STUDY NEXT?

## RECEIVING GOD'S GOODNESS

Imagine this. You're in a dungeon. Your cell is dark and dank. The floor is scattered with musty straw. Chains anchor you to the wall. There is no window — no glimpse of sky, no breath of fresh air. The only sounds you hear are the drip of condensation off bare stone and the rustle of rats. You crouch in the corner — listless, hopeless, defeated. Then you hear something unexpected — the crash of a distant door, the clamor of running feet. A key scrapes in the door to your cell, and the door swings open. There stands a rescuer, a knight in shining armor. He bends down and removes your chains and lifts you to your feet. "Come, let's get you out of here." But you pull away and back against the wall. "There must be some mistake. You must be looking for some other prisoner." With a tilt of the head, He asks, "And why do you think that?" Shrugging, you reply, "Well, because I committed a crime. I'm guilty. I deserve to be here. You should be looking for someone who is innocent, and doesn't belong here at all." With a nod of understanding, He takes your hand, "I know all that, but it's you I've come for. Don't you want to be free? I have come to set you free."

Unexpected mercy. God, in His goodness, sent Jesus to set the captives free. We were guilty, deserving of death, and living without hope when the door swung open. Unmerited favor. Jesus made it possible for our crimes to be forgiven, for our guilty verdict to be overturned, for our record to be wiped clean. Grace. The happy ending we didn't deserve.

In this study, we'll go from the prison of sin to the freedom and hope that is ours through the amazing grace of God. We never deserved God's goodness, and yet He extended it to us. All we had to do was receive it!

## EXPERIENCING SPIRITUAL INTIMACY

Some of my favorite storylines are about a guy and two different women. The first gal is always the guy's best bud. They've known each other since forever. He's comfortable with her, tells her everything, trusts her completely. In return, she's loved him since as long as she can remember, but he's never noticed. Then the second woman comes into the picture, and the guy is head over heels. In these stories, the first gal is usually stuck in the position of confidant, comforter, and even messenger to the new lady love. But for love of her guy, she sets aside her own feelings and does what he asks of her. In the end, the guy's eyes are opened somehow and he sees his dear friend in a new light. Startled to find love so close at hand, he berates himself for never really seeing her before. And, of course, they live happily ever after.

Many of us are blind to what is closest to us. In our hearts we long to experience spiritual intimacy. We want to know God and be known by Him. We long to see Jesus face-to-face, hear His voice, and touch His hand. We want to be close to God. We long to be His child, His beloved, His friend. We say we need a confidant and a comforter. Someone to trust and to tell our secrets to. We want God as our intimate—our up-close and personal friend. And in our yearning to be acknowledged by the Father and welcomed by the Son, we completely miss what is right in front of us. Right inside us, actually.

Do you know the treasure that is already hidden in your heart? Are you aware of the riches that are already yours? Those of us who are longing for spiritual intimacy need to have our eyes opened. The God we long to be close to is already closer than any sister, friend, or lover can ever be. God, in the Third Person. God, the Holy Spirit, dwells in us. Do you long for spiritual intimacy? This study opens up your eyes to the Spirit's role in our lives. He knows us in intimate ways. Get to know Him!

# LEADER'S GUIDE

## Chapter 1

**1.** "Who has **woe**? Who has **sorrow**? Who has **contentions**? Who has **complaints**? Who has **wounds** without **cause**? Who has **redness** of **eyes**?" (Prov. 23:29 NKJV).

**2.** "All joy is darkened, The mirth of the land is gone" (Is. 24:11 NKJV). There are many verses like this throughout the Old Testament. "Joy is dried up and withered in the hearts of the people" (Joel 1:12 MSG). When God's people were separated from God by their rebellion, their joy turned to ashes. They sank into joyless living.

**3.** "The mirth of the tambourine ceases, The noise of the jubilant ends, The joy of the harp ceases" (Is. 24:8 NKJV). When joy is absent, joyful noises disappear. There is no music, no song, no singing.

**4.** "I will put an end to the sound of your songs, and the sound of your harps shall be heard no more" (Ezek. 26:13 NKJV). Songs and music cease. "We hung our harps Upon the willows" (Ps. 137:2 NKJV). In their sadness, the captive people of God gave up their music.

**5.** "Behold, My servants shall sing for joy of heart, But you shall cry for sorrow of heart, And wail for grief of spirit" (Is. 65:14 NKJV). For those who do not belong to God, there is only one future—joyless living. But God's own children, His servants, His people—their lives will be characterized by joy. When we are God's, we are given the gift of a joyful heart.

**6.** "Make me hear joy and gladness" (Ps. 51:8 NKJV). We can ask the Lord to refresh our joyful outlook on life. He is able to make us glad.

**7.** "The heart knows its own bitterness, And a stranger does not share its joy" (Prov. 14:10 NKJV). Sometimes you'll hear people say, "Well, that's between them and the Lord." Nothing could be truer. Even the most discerning, wise, empathetic people cannot really read what's in our hearts. The joys and bitterness we experience are uniquely ours. Only the Lord knows our hearts.

**8.** "You will show me the path of life; In Your presence is fullness of joy; At Your right hand are pleasures forevermore" (Ps. 16:11 NKJV). David asks the Lord to show him the path that leads to joy. "Show me Your ways, O LORD; Teach me Your paths" (Ps. 25:4 NKJV). Again, the psalmist asks the Lord, "Show me!" "Open my eyes, that

I may see Wondrous things from Your law" (Ps. 119:18 NKJV). With our eyes opened, we can find the path to joy.

**9.** "Weeping may endure for a night, But joy comes in the morning" (Ps. 30:5 NKJV). For the believer, there is no need to linger in joyless living. Though we may need God's help to see the path into joy again, we are promised that joy is in our future. Though we may be going through a dark night, the hope of morning is ahead.

# Chapter 2

**1.** "My face is flushed from weeping, And on my eyelids is the shadow of death" (Job 16:16 NKJV). "My eye has also grown dim because of sorrow" (Job 17:7 NKJV). "By sorrow of the heart the spirit is broken" (Prov. 15:13 NKJV). Weeping, sad eyes, broken-heartedness.

**2.** "He who continually goes forth weeping, Bearing seed for sowing, Shall doubtless come again with rejoicing, Bringing his sheaves with him" (Ps. 126:6 NKJV). Though we may begin in sorrow, we can end in joy and rejoicing.

**3.** "Break forth into joy, sing together, You waste places" (Is. 52:9 NKJV). Break into joy—sing!

**4.** "Then shall the virgin **rejoice** in the **dance**, And the young men and the old, together; For I will **turn** their **mourning** to **joy**, Will **comfort** them, And make them **rejoice** rather than **sorrow**" (Jer. 31:13 NKJV).

**5.** "The ransomed of the LORD shall return, And come to Zion with singing, With everlasting joy on their heads. They shall obtain joy and gladness, And sorrow and sighing shall flee away" (Is. 35:10 NKJV). Where there was sorrow, there will be singing. Our joy will be everlasting. Joy and gladness will drive away all sorrow and sighing. What an encouragement to anyone whose joy has faded somewhat.

**6.** "To console those who mourn in Zion, To give them beauty for ashes, The oil of joy for mourning, The garment of praise for the spirit of heaviness" (Is. 61:3 NKJV). The ashes of our life will be exchanged for beauty. The mourning will be traded for perfumed oils. The heaviness of depression will be put aside and a garment of praise given instead.

**7.** "For the LORD will comfort Zion, He will comfort all her waste places; He will make her wilderness like Eden, And her desert like the garden of the LORD; Joy and gladness will be found in it, Thanksgiving and the voice of melody" (Is. 51:3 NKJV).

Where our lives were like desert places, God offers to transform them into a beautiful garden, like Eden itself.

**8.** "Therefore with joy you will draw water From the wells of salvation" (Is. 12:3 NKJV). Joy is drawn from the same well in which we find salvation. When we are saved, joy is God's gift to us.

**9.** "Restore to me the joy of Your salvation, And uphold me by Your generous Spirit" (Ps. 51:12 NKJV). David asks God to restore the joy he found when he was saved. Only He is able to uphold it in our hearts.

# Chapter 3

**1.** "The good times of the wicked are short-lived; godless joy is only momentary" (Job 20:5 MSG). Though anyone can experience happiness, you could argue that only believers can know true joy. Joy is a gift from God, and we can rejoice because He offers the ultimate reason for rejoicing.

**2.** "The people who walked in darkness Have seen a great light; Those who dwelt in the land of the shadow of death, Upon them a light has shined. You have multiplied the nation And increased its joy; They rejoice before You According to the joy of harvest" (Is. 9:2–3 NKJV). This prophecy is full of before and after. Before, we see darkness and death. After, we have light, joy, and rejoicing.

**3.** "And you will have joy and gladness, and many will rejoice at his birth" (Luke 1:14 NKJV). I love the way it's paraphrased in *The Message*: "You're going to leap like a gazelle for joy, and not only you—many will delight in his birth" (MSG). Elizabeth knew this kind of joy, as well, for when she and Mary came together, she said, "The moment the sound of your greeting entered my ears, The babe in my womb skipped like a lamb for sheer joy" (Luke 1:44 MSG).

**4.** "Then the angel said to them, 'Do not be afraid, for behold, I bring you good tidings of great joy which will be to all people'" (Luke 2:10 NKJV). The angel brought a message of joy. "Good news!" News of such earth-shaking gladness that all the world would have joy in it.

**5.** "When they saw the star, they rejoiced with exceedingly great joy" (Matt. 2:10 NKJV). Wise men from faraway lands recognized the signs of the fulfillment of prophecy. They knew joy when they realized that the heavens celebrated the coming of a new King.

**6.** "The kingdom of heaven is like treasure hidden in a field, which a man found and hid; and for joy over it he goes and sells all that he has and buys that field" (Matt. 13:44 NKJV). Do you recognize the life you have in Christ for the treasure that it is? We discover joy when we realize how much we have to rejoice over. Like the man in this parable, we should be willing to trade anything for it.

**7.** "Most assuredly, I say to you that you will weep and lament, but the world will rejoice, and you will be sorrowful, but your sorrow will be turned into joy" (John 16:20 NKJV). I'm sure these words sounded strange and mysterious at the time. When Jesus was killed, the world rejoiced and the disciples only knew fear and sorrow. But then, that bitter grief turned to astonished joy. Jesus tried to tell them there was hope, even in the face of death. They just didn't understand what He was telling them.

**8.** "So they went out quickly from the tomb with fear and great joy, and ran to bring His disciples word" (Matt. 28:8 NKJV). The joy they felt was mingled with fear. Could they trust the happiness they were feeling? Could the impossible really have happened? *The Message* says, "The women, deep in wonder and full of joy…ran to tell the disciples" (Matt. 28:8). "But while they still did not believe for joy, and marveled…" (Luke 24:41 NKJV). Joy and wonder washed over the disciples as they saw Jesus again with their own eyes. "And they worshiped Him, and returned to Jerusalem with great joy" (Luke 24:52 NKJV). Joy, and not just any joy. *Great* joy!

**9.** "These who have turned the world upside down have come here" (Acts 17:6 NKJV). Christians, with their contagious joy, turned the whole known world on its head. The transformation wrought by Christ was undeniable, and so faith and joy spread.

# Chapter 4

**1.** "Let all those rejoice who put their trust in You; Let them ever shout for joy, because You defend them; Let those also who love Your name Be joyful in You" (Ps. 5:11 NKJV). We can put our trust in God and love His name. We can rejoice and shout for joy. David says we should be joyful in Him—the Lord who defends us.

**2.** "Therefore they shall come and sing in the height of Zion, Streaming to the goodness of the LORD….Their souls shall be like a well-watered garden, And they shall sorrow no more at all" (Jer. 31:12 NKJV). Those who love the Lord shall find their souls refreshed and flourishing, like a well-watered garden. Joy replaces sorrow, singing rises from our hearts.

**3.** Did God call to your heart when you were just a child? Can you see His hand protecting you and guiding you to Himself over the course of the years? Was the Lord patient and persistent in His wooing of you, or were you swept off your feet the first time you heard His story? Each of us discovered the Lord's love for us somehow, and that was the moment when we only had eyes for Him. That was the day joy found a home in our hearts.

**4.** "For God gives wisdom and knowledge and joy to a man who is good in His sight" (Eccl. 2:26 NKJV). God gives good things to us, and in this passage, Solomon lists just a few of the things which our Father bestows. Wisdom and knowledge are from God's hand, as is joy. God gives us joy!

**5.** "For he will not dwell unduly on the days of his life, because God keeps him busy with the joy of his heart" (Eccl. 5:20 NKJV). This is a pleasant bit of imagery. I like the wording—God keeps us busy with the joy in our hearts. No other busywork is needed. All other distractions can be set aside. The joy He places in our hearts will be sufficient for us. He's all we need.

**6.** "So you shall rejoice in every good thing which the LORD your God has given to you and your house" (Deut. 26:11 NKJV). We can indeed derive great joy in our salvation. But it seems our joy is being renewed day by day as we see the Lord at work in our lives. We can rejoice over every good thing the Lord has given to us. In our gratitude, joy abounds.

**7.** "My **heart rejoices** in the LORD; My horn is **exalted** in the LORD. I **smile** at my enemies, Because I **rejoice** in Your **salvation**" (1 Sam. 2:1 NKJV). This prayer of joyful thanksgiving is worth reading in a few other translations! "Then Hannah prayed: 'My heart rejoices in the LORD! Oh, how the LORD has blessed me! Now I have an answer for my enemies, as I delight in your deliverance" (NLT). "Hannah prayed: 'I'm bursting with God-news! I'm walking on air. I'm laughing at my rivals. I'm dancing my salvation'" (MSG). "Hannah prayed: 'The LORD has filled my heart with joy; I feel very strong in the LORD. I can laugh at my enemies; I am glad because you have helped me!'" (NCV).

**8.** "Your words were found, and I ate them, And Your word was to me the joy and rejoicing of my heart; For I am called by Your name, O LORD God of hosts" (Jer. 15:16 NKJV). We rejoice because of our salvation, and we rejoice over the good things God gives us, but we also rejoice over the discoveries we make in God's Word. Our

Bibles are a source of comfort and joy, for they are God's revelation to us. When we find His Word and devour it, it becomes a source of joy in our lives.

**9.** "And all the people went their way to eat and drink, to send portions and rejoice greatly, because they understood the words that were declared to them" (Neh. 8:12 NKJV). For the first time in years, the people not only heard God's Word, but had people explain it to them. They understood what God's message to them was, and it was a cause of great joy to all the people.

# Chapter 5

**1.** Let's consider the variations we find between translations: "I'll banish every sound of joy—singing, laughter, marriage festivities, genial workmen, candlelit suppers" (Jer. 25:10 MSG). "Moreover I will take from them the voice of mirth and the voice of gladness…the sound of the millstones and the light of the lamp" (NKJV). "I will take away your happy singing and laughter…Your businesses will fail, and all your homes will stand silent and dark" (NLT).

**2.** "For you shall go out with joy, And be led out with peace; The mountains and the hills Shall break forth into singing before you, And all the trees of the field shall clap their hands" (Is. 55:12 NKJV). Just think! All of God's creation responds to Him in ways we cannot imagine. In this verse, Isaiah says that the mountains and hills shall sing and the trees shall clap their hands.

**3.** "Let the heavens rejoice, and let the earth be glad; And let them say among the nations, 'The LORD reigns.' Let the sea roar, and all its fullness; Let the field rejoice, and all that is in it. Then the trees of the woods shall rejoice before the LORD, For He is coming to judge the earth" (1 Chron. 16:31–33 NKJV). What a list! The heavens and the earth, the sea and the fields, the trees in the woods—all proclaim the Lord's majesty.

**4.** "When the morning stars sang together, And all the sons of God shouted for joy" (Job 38:7 NKJV). The stars themselves sing a song of praise, and all the sons of God shout for joy.

**5.** "They sing to the tambourine and harp, And rejoice to the sound of the flute" (Job 21:12 NKJV). Musical instruments were added early on to the joy and rejoicing of people.

**6.** "Then I will go to the altar of God, To God my exceeding joy; And on the harp I will praise You, O God, my God" (Ps. 43:4 NKJV). The psalmist says he'll go to the altar of God in order to sing praise to God, accompanied by his harp. I like the fact, too, that David calls God his "exceeding joy."

**7.** "And now my head shall be lifted up above my enemies all around me; Therefore I will offer sacrifices of joy in His tabernacle; I will sing, yes I will sing praises to the LORD" (Ps. 27:6 NKJV). David says he will bring sacrifices of praise to the Lord. How can we do that? David says to just sing it! We can offer the Lord who gives us joy the rejoicing which flows from it!

**8.** "The voice of **joy** and the voice of **gladness**, the voice of the **bridegroom** and the voice of the **bride**, the voice of those who will say: '**Praise** the **Lord** of hosts, For the **Lord** is **good**, For His **mercy** endures **forever**'—and of those who will **bring** the **sacrifice** of **praise** into the **house** of the LORD" (Jer. 33:11 NKJV).

**9.** "Sing to Him a new song; Play skillfully with a shout of joy" (Ps. 33:3 NKJV). Sing to the Lord. Not only that, create a new song to sing before Him. Be inventive, be creative, be sincere. Every time He surprises you with a new reason for rejoicing, you can find a new way to give thanks for it! And while you're putting your new song into words, give it your all. Why? Because David urges us to play skillfully—giving the Lord our best.

## Chapter 6

**1.** "When they said, 'Let's go to the house of God,' my heart leaped for joy" (Ps. 122:1 MSG). Going to the Temple for worship with the rest of the Israelite community gave this psalmist joy. It was something he looked forward to with cheerful anticipation.

**2.** "When I remember these things, I pour out my soul within me. For I used to go with the multitude; I went with them to the house of God, With the voice of joy and praise, With a multitude that kept a pilgrim feast" (Ps. 42:4 NKJV). David remembers with fondness and longing the times when he joined the throngs headed to the Temple.

**3.** "Be glad in the LORD and rejoice, you righteous; And shout for joy, all you upright in heart" (Ps. 32:11 NKJV). Rejoice! Be glad! And in your gladness, shout for joy before the Lord.

**4.** "Let Your saints shout for joy" (Ps. 132:9 NKJV). In other translations, we find God's saints referred to as "your loyal servants" (NLT), "your people" (NCV), and "your worshipers" (MSG).

**5.** "The pastures are clothed with flocks; the valleys also are covered with grain; They shout for joy, they also sing" (Ps. 65:13 NKJV). The earth, its crops, and the animals—all of God's creation—sing and shout for joy. Not one is left out of the corporate praise.

**6.** "Then David spoke to the leaders of the Levites to appoint their brethren to be the singers accompanied by instrument of music, stringed instruments, harps, and cymbals, by raising the voice with resounding joy" (1 Chron. 15:16 NKJV). This appears to have been a great production, with both symphony and choir. Stringed instruments, percussion instruments, and a large contingent of Levites for the choir. Together, they raised a resounding sound of joy to the Lord.

**7.** "And all the people went up after him; and the people played the flutes and rejoiced with great joy, so that the earth seemed to split with their sound" (1 Kings 1:40 NKJV). The earth seemed to split at the sound of their praise! "Everyone joined the fanfare, the band playing and the people singing, the very earth reverberating to the sound" (MSG). "The celebration was so joyous and noisy that the earth shook with the sound" (NLT).

**8.** "That day they offered great sacrifices, and rejoiced, for God had made them rejoice with great joy; the women and children also rejoiced, so that the joy of Jerusalem was heard afar off" (Neh. 12:43 NKJV). When the men, women, and children joined their voices in joyful praise, the noise of it could be heard from far away. "That day they offered great sacrifices, an exuberant celebration because God had filled them with great joy. The women and children raised their happy voices with all the rest. Jerusalem's jubilation was heard far and wide" (MSG).

**9.** "Let them shout for joy and be glad, Who favor my righteous cause; And let them say continually, 'Let the LORD be magnified, Who has pleasure in the prosperity of His servant'" (Ps. 35:27 NKJV). We are invited to shout for joy and magnify the Lord. In other variations, the verse reads, "But give great joy to those who have stood with me in my defense. Let them continually say, 'Great is the LORD, who enjoys helping his servant'" (NLT). "But those who want the best for me, Let them have the last word—a glad shout!—and say, over and over and over, 'God is great—everything works together for good for his servant'" (MSG). I like this thought, that the last word will be a glad shout!

# Chapter 7

**1.** "We are hard pressed on every side, yet not crushed; we are perplexed, but not in despair; persecuted, but not forsaken; struck down, but not destroyed—always carrying about in the body the dying of the Lord Jesus, that the life of Jesus also may be manifested in our body" (2 Cor. 4:8–10 NKJV). Life really can be hard. But joy is unstoppable.

**2.** "I am overwhelmed with joy despite all our troubles" (2 Cor. 7:4 MSG). Paul's ministry was always running up against obstacles. But Paul refused to let his troubles overwhelm him. Instead, he says that in spite of all their troubles, it was joy that overwhelmed his soul.

**3.** "Immersed in tears, yet always filled with deep joy; living on handouts, yet enriching many; having nothing, having it all" (2 Cor. 6:10 MSG). This verse is a study in contradictions. "Our hearts ache, but we always have joy" (NLT). "As sorrowful, yet always rejoicing" (NKJV).

**4.** "Although great trouble accompanied the Word, you were able to take great joy from the Holy Spirit!—taking the trouble with the joy, the joy with the trouble" (1 Thess. 1:6 MSG). Sometimes joy must go hand in hand with the troubles we're experiencing. "Having received the word in much affliction" (NKJV). The troubles we face needn't dictate the amount of joy we experience. "You received the message with joy from the Holy Spirit in spite of the severe suffering it brought you" (NLT).

**5.** "Rejoice in that day and leap for joy! For indeed your reward is great in heaven, For in like manner their fathers did to the prophets" (Luke 6:23 NKJV). When we face trials and persecution, we should leap for joy. This seems odd, indeed. But the reason for our rejoicing is that our reward will be great. We're going through the same kinds of suffering that other men and women of God have endured for centuries.

**6.** "But the fruit of the Spirit is love, joy, peace, longsuffering, kindness, goodness, faithfulness, gentleness, and self-control" (Gal. 5:22–23 NKJV). Joy is indeed one of the fruits of the Spirit. It flourishes along with the other attributes of the Spirit-led life, like patience, kindness, and love.

**7.** "Strengthened with all might, according to His glorious power, for all patience and longsuffering with joy" (Col. 1:11 NKJV). Have you ever had to put up with someone who had a martyr complex? Ever had one yourself? It's true that we can grit our teeth and tough it out if we have to, but there is greater grace if patience and longsuffering can be endured with a measure of joy. Longsuffering with joy is a pleasant mingling.

**8.** "Therefore we do not **lose heart**. Even though our **outward** man is **perishing**, yet the **inward** man is being **renewed** day by day. For our **light** affliction, which is but for a **moment**, is **working** for us a far more **exceeding** and **eternal** weight of **glory**, while we do not **look** at the things which are **seen**, but at the things which are **not seen**. For the things which are seen are **temporary**, but the things which are not seen are **eternal**" (2 Cor. 4:16–18 NKJV).

**9.** "Let us not grow weary while doing good, for in due season we shall reap if we do not lose heart" (Gal. 6:9 NKJV). Even though we have eternal promises with God, it's the temporary, everyday things that get in our faces and cause us to lose sight of what's most important. Losing heart is like losing your joy. Paul prays that we won't grow weary in doing the good and right things because God will keep all His promises to us. Continue your service to God with joy steadying your course.

# Chapter 8

**1.** "**Serving** the Lord with all **humility**, with many **tears** and **trials**" (Acts 20:19 NKJV). "Now for a **little while**, if need be, you have been **grieved** by **various trials**" (1 Peter 1:6 NKJV). "My brethren, **count** it all **joy** when you **fall** into **various trials**" (James 1:2 NKJV).

**2.** "A woman, when she is in labor, has sorrow because her hour has come; but as soon as she has given birth to the child, she no longer remembers the anguish, for joy that a human being has been born into the world" (John 16:21 NKJV). The trials and sorrows we face in this world are real and intense, like the labor pains of a mother-to-be. But their duration is limited, and the joy that awaits us at the end of them makes them more bearable.

**3.** "Therefore you now have sorrow, but I will see you again and your heart will rejoice, and your joy no one will take from you" (John 16:22 NKJV). We are also looking forward to seeing Jesus again, and when that happens, we'll have a joy of everlasting proportions. Nothing can ever mar it or diminish its intensity. "When I see you again, you'll be full of joy, and it will be a joy no one can rob from you" (MSG).

**4.** "Looking unto Jesus, the author and finisher of our faith, who for the joy that was set before Him endured the cross, despising the shame, and has sat down at the right hand of the throne of God" (Heb. 12:2 NKJV). Jesus was willing to endure the pain, suffering, and shame of His crucifixion because of the promised joy that lay farther down that path. If He could face death, could we face lesser trials with the same determination?

**5.** "If we endure, We shall also reign with Him" (2 Tim. 2:12 NKJV). Those who live for the Lord and learn to count the trials we face as a joy will be rewarded with even greater joy. Someday, we will reign with Jesus in a new heaven and a new earth. "If we stick it out with him, we'll rule with him; If we turn our backs on him, he'll turn his back on us" (MSG).

**6.** c, e, a, f, b, d

**7.** "Not only that, but we also glory in tribulations, knowing that tribulation produces perseverance; and perseverance, character; and character, hope" (Rom. 5:3–4 NKJV). There's a purpose behind all those inconveniences we face. They're helping us to grow up. They're developing character in our lives. As we persevere, counting these trials as joy, we find that hope is strengthened in our hearts.

**8.** "The life-maps of God are right, showing the way to joy. The directions of God are plain and easy on the eyes" (Ps. 19:8 MSG). The course God sets for us is always right. The path He sets before us leads to joy. To put it another way, "The statutes of the Lord are right, rejoicing the heart; The commandment of the LORD is pure, enlightening the eyes" (NKJV).

**9.** "And God will wipe away every tear from their eyes; there shall be no more death; nor sorrow, nor crying. There shall be no more pain, for the former things have passed away" (Rev. 21:4 NKJV). "The old world and its evils are gone forever" (NLT). This is a hope and promise we can count on seeing fulfilled one day.

# Chapter 9

**1.** "That I may come to you with joy by the will of God, and may be refreshed together with you" (Rom. 15:32 NKJV). Paul was always looking forward to the chance to get together with believers he knew in faraway churches. These were people he'd met when establishing churches on his missionary journeys, and many of them were his own spiritual children.

**2.** "Yes, brother, let me have joy from you in the Lord; refresh my heart in the Lord" (Philemon 1:20 NKJV). In both this passage and the previous one, Paul mentions having his heart refreshed.

**3.** "Behold, how good and how pleasant it is For brethren to dwell together in unity!" (NKJV). The psalmist goes on in this short poem to compare this harmony to precious things—sacred anointing oils and the essential dews that brought life to such a dry land. Other versions are equally descriptive. "How wonderful, how beautiful, when brothers and sisters get along!" (MSG).

**4.** "The generous prosper and are satisfied; those who refresh others will themselves be refreshed" (Prov. 11:25 NLT). Or as the New King James Version puts it, "The generous soul will be made rich, And he who waters will also be watered himself" (NKJV). When it comes to community and the joy we share with one another, generosity is a must. If we're always worrying about whether we'll be acknowledged or appreciated for what we do, we're missing the point. God promises that those who refresh others will be refreshed in turn.

**5.** "Not that we have dominion over your faith, but are fellow workers for your joy; for by faith you stand" (2 Cor. 1:24 NKJV). Paul referred to himself and his friends as fellow workers for the faith and joy of believers. "And being confident of this, I know that I shall remain and continue with you all for your progress and joy of faith" (Phil. 1:25 NKJV). Paul stayed in the areas where new converts were made to help them grow in the faith. He stayed so that their joy and faith could be strengthened. "For what is our hope, or joy, or crown of rejoicing? Is it not even you in the presence of our Lord Jesus Christ at His coming? For you are our glory and joy" (1 Thess. 2:19–20 NKJV). People matter. They're one of the only things in this whole created world that will last for eternity. Paul knew this, and poured out his life for the sake of something everlasting. Every single person who turned to faith in Christ was a source of deep, lasting joy for Paul.

**6.** e, c, g, a, f, b, d

**7.** "A man has joy by the answer of his mouth, And a word spoken in due season, how good it is!" (Prov. 15:23 NKJV). "A person's words can be life-giving water; words of true wisdom are as refreshing as a bubbling brook" (Prov. 18:4 NLT). Our words are powerful tools. They can give great joy to others when we use them wisely. The right word, spoken at the right time, can be refreshing to another's heart.

**8.** "Now may the God of patience and comfort grant you to be like-minded toward one another, according to Christ Jesus, that you may with one mind and one mouth glorify the God and Father of our Lord Jesus Christ" (Rom. 15:5–6 NKJV). As another translation phrases it, "Then we'll be a choir—not our voices only, but our very lives singing in harmony in a stunning anthem to the God and Father of our Master Jesus!" (MSG). What a beautiful word picture. The harmony of our lives in relationship with other believers becomes worship before God.

**9.** "Finally, brethren, farewell. Become complete. Be of good comfort, be of one mind, live in peace; and the God of love and peace will be with you all" (2 Cor. 13:11 NKJV). Other versions interject such encouragements as, "Be cheerful," "Keep your spirits up," "Think in harmony," and "Be agreeable" (MSG).

# Chapter 10

**1.** "To You, O my **Strength**, I will **sing praises**" (Ps. 59:17 NKJV). "I shall be **glorious** in the **eyes** of the **Lord**, And My **God** shall be My **strength**" (Is. 49:5 NKJV).

**2.** g, c, d, b, a, e, f

**3.** "He said to me, 'My grace is sufficient for you, for My strength is made perfect in weakness.' Therefore most gladly I will rather boast in my infirmities, that the power of Christ may rest upon me" (2 Cor. 12:9 NKJV). Sometimes, God's strength doesn't show up in our lives unless we're confronted with a situation in which we feel totally helpless. When we're at the end of ourselves, He carries us on in His strength. When we are the weakest, we depend on Him the most.

**4.** "Do not sorrow, for the joy of the LORD is your strength" (Neh. 8:10 NKJV). According to this verse, God isn't our only source of power. Our joy in the LORD also lends us strength.

**5.** "The king shall have joy in Your strength, O LORD" (Ps. 21:1 NKJV). The strength of the LORD brings joy. "How the king rejoices in your strength, O LORD! He shouts with joy because of your victory" (NLT). Or to paraphrase it even further, "Your strength, God, is the king's strength. Helped, he's hollering Hosannas" (MSG).

**6.** "These things I have spoken to you, that My joy may remain in you, and that your joy may be full" (John 15:11 NKJV). Jesus wanted to give us joy, to leave us with joy. That joy is a part of our spiritual strength now. And this isn't just joy, but a full and mature joy. "I've told you these things for a purpose: that my joy might be your joy, and your joy wholly mature" (John 15:11 MSG).

**7.** "You have multiplied the nation And increased its joy; They rejoice before You According to the joy of harvest" (Is. 9:3 NKJV). Joy isn't necessarily just there in our lives. It's vital and vibrant, able to surge into greater abundance. The Lord can increase our joy. "The humble also shall increase their joy in the LORD, and the poor among men shall rejoice in the Holy One of Israel" (Is. 29:19 NKJV). Our joy in the Lord can be increased! More joy!

**8.** "These things I speak in the world, that they may have My joy fulfilled in themselves" (John 17:13 NKJV). So often the Word leads to joy of heart. Even here, Jesus speaks so that those who hear Him can experience the fullness of joy. "I'm saying these things in the world's hearing So my people can experience My joy completed in them" (MSG). Jesus was very intentional in the giving of joy to His followers. He knew how much they would need the strength it offers to our faith and our feelings.

**9.** "You will show me the path of life; In Your presence is fullness of joy; At Your right hand are pleasures forevermore" (Ps. 16:11 NKJV). The joy we experience now is good and pure and strengthening. But it's nothing compared to the joy that awaits us in the Lord's presence. There we will know a fullness of joy unimaginable.

# Chapter 11

**1.** What wonderful imagery! Joy is better than shopping sprees! It has us running and jumping and laughing and whistling. Joy makes us feel ten feet tall—strong and invincible. We feel like turning cartwheels, and our lives are so abundantly blessed, they brim over with even greater joy.

**2.** "Then you shall see and become radiant, And your heart shall swell with joy" (Is. 60:5 NKJV). Shining faces, shining eyes. You can always tell a joyful person by the radiant glow on their faces.

**3.** "...Rejoices like a strong man to run its race" (Ps. 19:5 NKJV). "It bursts forth like a radiant bridegroom after his wedding. It rejoices like a great athlete eager to run the race" (NLT). There's a joy in doing what God made us to do. This verse reminds me of Eric Liddel, the *Chariots of Fire* guy, who said, "God made me fast...and when I run I feel God's pleasure."

**4.** "O God, enthroned above the cherubim, display your radiant glory" (Ps. 80:1 NLT). What a beautiful description of God. "You who dwell between the cherubim, shine forth!" (NKJV). "You sit on your throne between the gold creatures with wings." (NCV). "Throw beams of light from your dazzling throne" (MSG).

**5.** "They looked to Him and were radiant, And their faces were not ashamed" (Ps. 34:5 NKJV). "Those who look to him for help will be radiant with joy; no shadow of shame will darken their faces" (NLT). Those who look to the Lord for His strength and help will be radiant with the joy He gives.

**6.** "They will come home and **sing songs** of **joy** on the heights of Jerusalem. They will be **radiant** because of the many **gifts** the LORD has given them....Their **life** will be like a **watered garden**, and all their **sorrows** will be **gone**" (Jer. 31:12 NLT).

**7.** "Then the righteous will shine forth as the sun in the kingdom of their Father" (Matt. 13:43 NKJV). It's a glowing promise. "Then the good people will shine like the sun" (NCV). "At the same time, ripe, holy lives will mature and adorn the kingdom of their father" (MSG).

**8.** "They bring life and radiant health to anyone who discovers their meaning" (Prov. 4:22 NLT). "Those who discover these words live, really live; body and soul, they're bursting with health" (MSG).

**9.** "If you are filled with light, with no dark corners, then your whole life will be radiant, as though a floodlight is shining on you" (Luke 11:36 NLT). Our whole lives can be radiant with light. "If then your whole body is full of light, having no part dark, the whole body will be full of light, as when the bright shining of a lamp gives you light" (NKJV). "Keep your life as well-lighted as your best-lighted room" (MSG).

# Chapter 12

**1.** "River fountains splash joy, cooling God's city, this sacred haunt of the Most High" (Ps. 46:4 MSG). "Always dreamed of a room in your house, where I could sing to joy to God-alive!" (Ps. 84:2 MSG). "My soul longs, yes, even faints For the courts of the LORD; My heart and my flesh cry out for the living God" (NKJV).

**2.** "Look ahead with joy. Anticipate what I'm creating: I'll create Jerusalem as sheer joy, create my people as pure delight" (Is. 65:18 MSG). "But be glad and rejoice forever in what I create" (NKJV). "Be glad; rejoice forever in my creation! And look! I will create Jerusalem as a place of happiness. Her people will be a source of joy" (NLT). The future holds many sources of joy. God will remake things, and the new city and people He creates will be sheer joy.

**3.** "It shall **blossom** abundantly and **rejoice**, Even with **joy** and **singing**" (Is. 35:2 NKJV). "Be **glad** and **rejoice forever** in what I create; For behold, I create Jerusalem as a **rejoicing**, And her people a **joy**. I will **rejoice** in Jerusalem, And **joy** in My people; The voice of weeping shall no longer be heard in her, Nor the voice of crying" (Is. 65:18–19 NKJV).

**4.** "Whom having not seen you love. Though now you do not see Him, yet believing, you rejoice with joy inexpressible and full of glory" (1 Peter 1:8 NKJV). We love the Lord, and we believe in Him even though we haven't ever seen Him. Because of this, we receive inexpressible joy.

**5.** "You have made known to me the ways of life; You will make me full of joy in Your presence" (Acts 2:28 NKJV). The fullness of joy can only be found in the presence of the Lord.

**6.** "He shall pray to God, and He will delight in him, He shall see His face with joy, For He restores to man His righteousness" (Job 33:26 NKJV). We shall know pure joy when we see God's face.

**7.** "But rejoice to the extent that you partake in Christ's sufferings, that when His glory is revealed, you may also be glad with exceeding joy" (1 Peter 4:13 NKJV). Peter looks forward to the very same event we do. He says our joy will be exceedingly great on the day when Jesus returns in all His glory.

**8.** "Well done, good and faithful servant; you were faithful over a few things, I will make you ruler over many things. Enter into the joy of your lord" (Matt. 25:21 NKJV). These are the very words we long to hear—"Well done, good and faithful servant." But have you ever noticed that last bit before? "Enter into the joy of your Lord." There it is! We will enter joy someday!

**9.** "Now to Him who is able to keep you from stumbling, And to present you faultless Before the presence of His glory with exceeding joy" (Jude 1:24 NKJV). We'll be there together, entering joy. Forever joy. Eternal joy. Exceedingly great joy.

# THE COMPLETE WOMEN OF FAITH®
## STUDY GUIDE SERIES

# NELSON IMPACT

## A Division of Thomas Nelson Publishers

### *Since 1798*

The Nelson Impact Team is here to answer your questions and suggestions as to how we can create more resources that benefit you, your family, and your community.

Contact us at Impact@thomasnelson.com